811
HoL
c.1

Chicks Up Front

D0878433

Learning Center
Twin Groves Junior High School
2600 Buffalo Grove Rd.
Buffalo Grove, IL. 60089

DISCARD

Chicks up front

poems by

Sara Holbrook

DISCARD

Learning Center
Twin Groves Junior High School
2600 Buffalo Grove Rd.
Buffalo Grove, IL 60089

Copyright © 1998 by Sara Holbrook

ISBN 1-880834-39-1

Cleveland State University Poetry Center
imagination series

All Rights Reserved. No part of this publication may be produced, stored in a retrieval system, or transmitted in any form or by any means, electronic, mechanical, photocopying, recording, or otherwise, without the prior written permission of the publisher. Printed in the United State of America.

Cleveland State University
1983 East 24th Street
Cleveland, OH 44115-2440
(216) 687-3986

This book is dedicated to
Christie Kushner
... for talking me down
and Katie and Kelly
... forever.

Many thanks to David Lackey and my friends at
Strongsville High School for inspiration and
editing, to Anna Reuben for cover design, to
Martin Reuben for photography, to Dr. Neal
Chandler and the staff at the CSU Poetry Center,
to Jane Toma and Len Toma at Herwell Press, and
to Marc Smith for getting me started and helping
me over the finish line on this book.

other books by Sara Holbrook

Juvenile

Am I Naturally This Crazy?
The Dog Ate My Homework
I Never Said I Wasn't Difficult
Which Way to the Dragon
Nothing's the End of the World
(Boyds Mills Press)

What's So Big About Cleveland, Ohio
(Gray & Company)

Contents

Chicks Up Front

Chicks Up Front

Before and After, we stand separate,
stuck to the same beer-soaked floor,
fragranced, facing the same restroom mirror.
Adjusting loose hairs — mine brown, hers purple.
Fumbling for lipsticks — mine pink, hers black —
a color I couldn't wear anyway since that convention of lines
gathered around my mouth about a year ago, won't leave.
We avoid eye contact; both of us are afraid of being carded.

Mature, I suppose I should speak, but what can I say
to the kind of hostility that turns hair purple and lips black?
Excuse me, I know I never pierced my nose,
but hey, I was revolting once, too.
Back . . . before I joined the PTA,
when Wonder Bras meant , "where'd I put that."
I rebelled against the government system,
the male-female system, the corporate system, you name it.
I marched, I chanted, I demonstrated.
And when shit got passed around,
I was there, sweetheart, and I inhaled.
Does she know that tear gas
makes your nose run worse than your eyes?
Would she believe that I was a volunteer
when they called "chicks up front?"
Because no matter what kind of hand-to-hand combat
the helmeted authoritarians may have been engaged in at home,
they were still hesitant to hit girls with batons in the streets.
"CHICKS UP FRONT!"
And we marched, and we marched,
and we marched right back home:

Where we bore the children
we were not going to bring into this mad world,
and we brought them home to the houses
we were never going to wallpaper in those Laura Ashley prints,
and we joined the corporate mongers
we were not going to let supervise our lives,
where we skyrocketed to middle-management positions
accepting less money than
we were never going to take anyway
and spending it on the Barbie Dolls
we were not going to buy for our daughters.

And after each party for our comings and goings,
we whisked the leftovers into dust pans,
debriefing and talking each other down from the drugs
and the men as if they were different.
Resuscitating one another as women do,
mouth to mouth.
That some of those who we put up front
really did get beaten down and others now bathe
themselves daily in Prozac to maintain former freshness.

Should I explain what tedious work it is putting role models together
and how sometimes strategic pieces get sucked up by this vacuum?
And while we intended to take one giant leap for womankind,
I wound up taking one small step, alone.

What can I say
at that moment our eyes meet in the mirror,
which they will.
What can I say to purple hair, black lips and a nose ring?
What can I say?

"Take care."

If I Were a Poem

If I were a poem,
I would grab you by the ankles
and rustle you up to your every leaf.
I would gather your branches
in the power of my winds and pull you skyward,
if I were a poem.

If I were a poem,
I would walk you down beside the rushing stream,
swollen with spring, put thunder in your heart,
then lay you down, a new lamb, to sing you to softly sleep,
if I were a poem.

If I were a poem,
I wouldn't just talk to you of politics, society and change,
I would be a raging bonfire to strip you of your outer wrap,
and then I would reach within and with one touch
ignite the song in your own soul.

If I were a poem,
I would hold my lips one breath away from yours
and inflate you with such desire as can exist
only just out of reach, and then I would move
the breadth of one bee closer, not to sting,
but to brush you with my wings as I retreat
to leave you holding nothing but a hungry, solitary sigh,
if I were a poem.

If I were a poem,
my thoughts would finally be put to words
through your own poetry, I would push you that far,
if I were a poem.

Naked

The first time I saw a man naked,
it was not my brother.
I was born without a brother,
which everyone knows
is like being born without green hair,
or a wart on the tip of your nose.
or the skin of a reptile.
Being born with no brother was a definite asset,
or so I thought until fifth grade, when I started to wonder.
I wondered why every time I would mention the word "it,"
in any context,
the boys would laugh — they'd fall on the ground.
Likewise, if I would say the word "them,"
in any context, the boys would laugh — they'd fall on the ground.
It was as if we were tuned into two different programs,
like they were tuned into cartoons
and I was watching a mystery.
I wondered.
And I wondered with the sense of urgency
of 4:30 in the afternoon and Mom says,
"No more snacks before dinner,"
and you're starving.
I wanted what I wanted and I wanted it now.

Prevailing neighborhood trade policies
provided for such things,
a look for a look, even up.
Worth considering,
until a permission slip came home from school.
There was to be a film about growing up.

Well, even I knew that was fiftiespeak for "naked."
My wonder swelled within me —
I had swallowed a balloon.
I couldn't breathe.
Breathless, until the film showed us diagrams.
Diagrams? Bones without the meat.
It looked like a direction sheet on how to assemble a bicycle,
absolutely no help at all. I deflated gradually.
A couple weeks later, another film.
No permission slip this time.
Just a film about the war of our fathers, World War II.
Germany. Hitler youth. Wind up soldiers.
    Waving train cars.
        Pits of white, white limbs.   Ovens, not for cakes.
            Three men standing against a fence, heads shaved.
            Their collar bones poking out like
                coat hangers without the clothes.
                The picture cut off at the hollow places where
                    their bellies belonged.
                Except for one man, standing in the background,
                    who stepped deliberately to the side.
                Stripped of any sense of wonder or urgency,
                    he made no attempt to cover himself.
                He faced the camera because he wanted me to see.

                    I dragged my feet a little on the way
                        home from school that day,
                    kicking aimlessly at the fallen leaves.
                        Not so much in a hurry.
                        After all, I had seen.
                        For the first time,
                        I had seen a man,
                                naked.

Close Companions

Passion is
the companion
    of youth
running with fools
    like trust
    and truth...
believing the promise
    of hope
    and wish,
flirting
    with love,
racing
    with risk.

Growing up is
a cold, hard trade,
    if maturity's
        only companion
           is age.

One, Taken to Heart ...

for Wendy

A book,
so much a part of our lives, seems lost.
Fallen, somewhere, out of place.
We drag about the house in heavy shoes,
examining the empty room.
We open the blinds, wash our eyes, and search the shelf for answers.
Thinking:
What could I have done with that book?
Where did I see it last?
Could a book just wander off like that?
Questions to throw at the moon,
while standing rooted in the shadows,
remembering the story.

The story.
Remember the time?
        The page?
                The chapter?
Remember?
Remember the smile?
A book can get lost, disappear, or simply fall to pieces,
but a story plays forever once we've taken it to heart.
And for the rest of what each of us will know of eternity,
whenever we drag about the house in heavy shoes,
wash our eyes, and search the shelf for answers,
that story will survive to coax us from the empty room
and back into the moonlight:
A sister,
teaching us to dance.

How to Write a Love Poem

To write a love poem
is to bring the length of chaos into shortened lines.
It is a cataloging of the unutterable, a labeling of sighs,
a flirtation with the tritely sentimental,
a marking off of starts, a polishing of finishes.
It is making love, no hands.

Naturally, it helps to be symptomatic,
preferably yearning or dwindling,
for at the crest of the wave,
who is inclined toward holding just a pen?
But, where do you go if all those breathless symptoms now throb
with the cold, rough bones of last summer's corn
at the bottom of the compost heap of memory?
How do you reorder them for recollection?
Further, how do you project them onto someone else's understanding?
How do you write a love poem?

Since none ever arrived general delivery,
you must first purchase a ticket
to a specific place without agent, cash or credit.
Send a telegram to one you've yet to meet,
and invite him to that spot
you can't ever say you've never been before, again.
Let her set the date.
Never agree to a time and try, try not to show up late.
Now wait.

Not even for a moment, pack your bag, leave it behind.
Jump the outbound train, never leave your desk,
carefully define your limits, always answer, "yes."
Record the sweep of every sunset, forget it with the dawn,
research these facts endlessly, then, make it up as you go along.
Since travel is unlimited, confine yourself,
to one stone balcony in — Spain.
When the audience of stars is seated,
promise never to rhyme, a — a —

10

Love is death warmed over to those of us over seventeen.
It was killed by the schemes and the patterns and revived by the tides.
It is the wisdom of the senseless to open up a heart,
a surgery of your naked self.
Its poetry, the pieces, offered about to make us whole.

So, here, take this pebble
and place it in the door before it clicks completely closed.
And strip. Go on. Go stand naked on that balcony.
Smell the songs as they lift themselves from the festival below.
Listen for the gardenias, and find that single, slender spot
still warm from the day's gone sun.

Now, take your paper.
And without detriment of pen, record the complete history of time,
of your life and of your parents, in your choicest words.
Brace yourself against the stone wall
and throw the paper into the street.

Focus
            on the
dizzy,
            drifting
paper.
            Feel the falling.
But not the fall.
Inhale yourself upright, but not around, and lifting
the hair from your nape with the rotation of both wrists,
stand still as the moon.

The poem will come
and kiss you
on the neck.

11

Raspberries

For once, for once...
to take love slowly
as the blossoms on the vine
spring between the thorns
past seasons left behind.

To wait . . .
as velvet-hearted flowers
reflecting colors of the sun,
are carried off by warming breezes,
petals dropping one by one.

To wait . . .
as they're replaced by coming berries,
small and hard,
that time permitting, grow,
trusting in the summer
to let their colors show.

To wait . . .
taking comfort in the days,
the roots, the rain, the heat,
to ripen this time slowly.
To taste,
full grown and sweet.

Strictly Business

Do not dream.
Never.
Not a flight of fancy, no imagery,
no pretending other faces, other voices,
other hands. God no.
Strictly business.
Focus. Prepare yourself.
You must corral all the wild horses,
circle wagons, batten down.
No loose shingles of the mind.
Latch the screen and lock the door.
Do not dream.

Have you ever sold yourself for money?
Not your time, your skills, your talents.
Your self. The one you got born with.
The skin. The muscle.
Your bones.
Have you sold it for money?
Ever?

It is a living; but do the living after.
The trick is . . . there is a trick . . .
they call it a trick.
The trick is not to play dead.
The trick is to be dead but play alive.
They always want a response.
Like a child banging away on a piano,
he thinks he hears a song
because the keys respond, they make noise.
The song only exists in his head,
but that's enough to keep the
child banging away.

13

Focus.
On your every movement, his response.
His movement, your response.
Let him pay the price, not you.
Prepare yourself. Chill.
Don't worry. In these waters you won't turn blue.
He'll never know as long as you just play along.

Other women work in worse conditions,
they stand in freezers gutting fish.
Some pick thorny roses with bleeding hands,
the pesticides giving them cancers.
Do you think they feel every little prick?
Some women simply trade their candy for a wrapper,
designer jeans, split level house.
These women have worked *hard* to maintain the
high patina of numbness required for the job.
Days, shifts, hours, decades.
Forget the bragging,
this job will take you only a few minutes.
You can do it.

But do not dream.
Hands can pass over you again and again
and feel only numbness,
but a dream can touch you beneath the callous of reality,
and it might press the wrong keys.
This is a dangerous piece of equipment
you are operating here.
You don't want it to start eating you piece by piece.
No matter the temptation for escape.
No matter the boredom.
Remember — strictly business.
Prepare yourself. Focus.
Do not dream.

We Own This Town

(a poem for two voices)

From downtown to the suburbs, the streets are mine.
People complain, but they all want me to do what I do.
Stores get insurance claims, people have someone to blame
and cops get to keep their jobs.

So you want to be one of the gang down at the Union Club.
Boy, you've got to change your colors.
Our colors are gray and white.

I do what I'm forced to do. If I had other options
I'd make other choices, but now, I choose to survive.

It's survival of the fittest, downtown,
no welfare programs here, it's natural selection.
We are the corporate heads and out of our hats come
the names of who and what's going to work in this town.
Need a building? A stadium? Done!

If I put a gun to your head, I can take what you own.
If I want power, I take power.   Done!

Not give and take, take and give.
We are benevolent dictating contributions to the ballet,
good public relations.
Not food banks, son. Poor writeoffs just don't make good press.

Damn the press and Ted Koppel.
I rob from the rich and give to poor little ol' me.
I even got a crew, everybody needs a Board of Trustees.
Nobody can fight the world alone.
You might not respect us even in numbers,
so we carry bullets and chrome.

15

Together. One for all and all for us.
Power! We own this town, everybody's on our turf.
I can't afford to be soft-hearted, it's kill or be killed,
there are no POWs coming out of this war.
And the money? It's just a way of keeping score.

>Money ain't nothin' to a dead man,
>so you better check the body count.
>We didn't ask for war, you gave it to us.
>So either shit or get off the pot.
>I have to be true to the game,
>compassion in battle will get a brother shot.

Come on over here and meet our homeboys —
best part is, we hardly ever go home.
Hey you! Use the back steps.
You look good in the bedroom, but not in the board room,
this way to the ladies waiting room, miss.

>And all you bitches can wait until hell freezes over.
>'Cause if your baby dies? If you die? If a cop dies?
>And I don't die? Everything is fine.
>When all competition is gone, the game will be over,
>and the world will be mine. In Guns We Trust.

Our motto is: In Tradition We Trust.
And speaking of trust, son, put down that gun.
That's no way to rob a bank.

Indented verses written by Anthony C. Rucker, 'Da Boogieman.

Democracy

My office is government issue.
The basics, one metal desk, one chair, a stack of folders,
four rubber stamps and a whole lot of paper
in need of baling wire, or a match.
A gray office beside a multicolored room
full of folks waiting on government basics.

Thump.
Thump.
A large woman thumps, thumps.
Thumps past my office.
Thump. Thump, down the hall to the ladies room.
Sounds of running water, a squeaky door slaps against the wall
and oozes toward a bumpy close.
Thump. Thump. I look up as she passes again.
Dark hallway.
Dark clothing.
White toilet paper.
Thump. Thump.
I watch after her passing.
Thump. Thump.
She stole the toilet paper.
Also government issue, two rolls per day.

Issued by the same government that will
murder a mountain of forest for the confusion
of paper it takes to purchase a pencil through
proper procurement procedures.
The same government that offers tax abated housing to
for-profit football teams and levies income tax on
where's-the-profit unemployment compensation.

The same government that issues food stamps for
koolaid, popsicles, and tater tots, but not for toilet paper,
like it's some privilege that poor folks don't need.
That same government issues us two rolls per day,
94% of the days since our last 6% cut.
Two rolls.

I rub at the crow's feet, which are deepening into my mother's face.
She stole the toilet paper.
The clock silently mouths that it's just 3:05.
I wait for a moment, reluctant to go once more against the mountain,
knowing the thin air makes me lightheaded.
Finally I move.

"Ma'am, did you take our toilet paper?"
She looks straight ahead, two rolls propped on knees flung wide.
She is slow to acknowledge my presence,
slow looking up at the self-conscious stand I have taken
beside her over-filled chair in this over-filled room.
And then, in a glance, she reminds me that I am too tall,
too thin, too well-dressed, and too goddamned white.

"I need it," she replies.
And that need, I know, is not entirely selfish,
that need embraces the needs of her children,
her grandchildren, maybe a neighbor.
But it does not embrace the needs of the neighbors
with whom she shares this waiting room.
"I have to ask for it back," I say, citing the needs of the others.
Reluctant herself, she complies.
Practically speaking, she *is* a republican.
I retreat to return the basics to the necessary place,
dizzy with democracy.

May I Have Your Order, Please?

Well, wrap me in ruffles and curl my hair,
will you look at that one on page two.
Not the dress, not the dress, but that dreamfeed in denim,
that bulge in the breakaway shirt.
That one with the locks and the rocks
(oh my socks) and the grin and the come-hither eyes.
The one that goes in where he's belted
with nothing left over, the man in the flannel,
life can't be worth living without.

Without him, darling, *him*.
The one in the middle, shoes pictured on page 56.
Oh, there's no mercy. None at all.
Not when we can't order up men from a catalog.
Give me that, one of those and that, too.
Size?
I'll take extra large, please, in color choice D.
Here's my number, wrap and express, lord have mercy.
I'll wait on the step.

Ah, there's no justice.
None at all, not when so much of life comes to us
through one of those wee little cocktail straws
and most of us just dying of thirst.
Which is why we are willing to pay a hundred, at least,
(don't be cheap) for a dress, eighty for a scarf and
sixteen for a lipstick to match, just in case we might meet,
by chance at the coffee shop, that someone who
always comes early or late.

Oh, yes, I know the virtues of patience.
Don't we all. Haven't we just all just said no, not without sunscreen?
Haven't we lived on water and cuticle diets?
Haven't we delayed gratification one more night
till our underwear matched?
Haven't we waited for door bells and phone calls
and foot falls and whatalls that come from men
who want what they want when they want it
but not when they don't and we're supposed to guess?
Haven't we caught ourselves, tapping our feet, desperate to dance,
watching for the silhouette of that someone who's coming to ask,
taking good care to be shaved, just in case,
manicured, lip-lined and blushed?

We want and we want and we want with a passion,
and goddamn it, we're going to look good while we're waiting
and sip-sip-sipping. Well, my shoes are so full up with patience
I'm goddamn near stuck to this floor.
I say it's time I grabbed the rooster by the throat
and crowed on my time, for my time has dawned.
I got my carry-on packed for carrying on,
all I need is a man on the side.

So, if I can't have Mr. Flannel looking so tight in the pockets,
well, then, damn it, better send me the dress.
'Cause if I can't pick him, then he'll have to pick me and bygod,
I'm going to be needing the dress.
He would love me in that color.
He would love me in that color.
Watch me move in the fashion he loves.
If I can't have one of those, then I'll take one of these.
I need that dress now,
Please. Please. Please.

Bachelor

Bachelor,
your prelude's
a double-step stomp on my doorstep.
    No knock. Just a perfunctory
    two-step to knock off the dirt.
Easier than covering your tracks,
    I presume.
    Polite, if only by chance.
Oh, you are here
    by chance,
    not by prior commitment.
Not a commitment, not from
    a man who thinks
    a knock before entry is
planning too far in advance.
    Stomp. Stomp.
    And the swing of the door.
And what do we call this?
    Not, "just passing through," that's for strangers
    and all of your strangeness, I know.
Certainly not,
    "the man returns home."
    This is not your address.
An entry is all, announced only by your absence —
    it's been a few days and
    it's time.
Abrupt. Your entry is as dry as too cold snow
    blowing in on a draft,
    resistant to holding.
Not a word, no promises made or implied.
    Not a touch, not a stroke,
    not a kiss on the nose.

Not even a gratuitous pause in the foyer.
     For even a pause
     would hold too much intimacy in its palm.
A spectator, I follow,
     lagging as usual,
     a few steps behind.
Familiar as I am with this shortcut style of yours,
     I'm hesitant.
     Shortcuts can hurt.
Without excuses you plunge directly into the warmth
     of my kitchen.
     Deeper. Deeper.
Into the pantry, where I keep all the stuff that makes men
     grow stronger and faster. Peering. Wordless.
     Hungry again are you? For what?
You gaze at all the food you've passed over before.
     The soups that might feel warm to the tongue,
     The noodles that might boil into softness.
The sweet berry jams.
     And the rice, of course the rice.
     It takes 25 minutes.
You grab for the quick-fixing
     peanut butter
     and screw till it opens.
Without pretense of utensils
     you plunge again and again
     into the thick resistance of the jar.
Still watching, I pull open a drawer,
     looking in to where I have
     printed and taped a clear message:
DON'T FALL FOR THAT BEGGAR AGAIN.
     I reach into the drawer
     and hand you a knife.

Watch Out!

Watch out!
The alarm is set on her body clock,
like Hook's crocodile, you can hear "tick tock,"
. . . and he just wants to get laid.

Watch out!
She has a leg-hold trap, baited, in her purse,
divorced with children, what could be worse?
. . . and he just wants to get laid.

She needs a father figure, furs, a car.
She's mad as hell. She's twice as hard,
. . . and he, he just —

Experience warns us that love is not true,
it never boils down to just me and you.
There are parents.
Past loves.
Under those covers the mixture's explosive.
Every crime of passion requires a motive.

He's on the rebound.
She can't commit.
He can't open his eyes to kiss.
That's it!
He's broken. She's damaged.
He's angry. She's torn.
Both of their hearts are calloused and worn.

Break this romance addiction.
Stop infatuation.
All this could be cured
with the right
medication.

Try TV.   Try beer.
Try ice cream. Try drugs.
E-mail your intimates.
Chat rooms, group hugs.
"Play it safe."
"Play it cool."
Don't get, "played for a fool."
Buy flannel sheets.
Meditate in the dark.
Turn up the music!
That crying you hear is only your heart,
and it doesn't make sense.
So, don't go near that door.
For one breath of that sea breeze . . .
    for one taste of that berry . . .
        for one palm to palm touch . . .
      moist . . .
you'll only want more.

                              Watch out!

Let's Not Burn the House Down

Look,
I don't want to burn the house down.
You can't strike me like some match,
hold me in the dark
and expect that fire to catch.
No, I've had enough of that
heartburned misery, enough of me left smoldering,
face dirt-streaked with rain, waiting on an ambulance
to come collect my pain.

I've given at the office,
I've given them the door.
I've even given out fat chances,
and now you want me to give some more?
Out of which account?
My Love's way overdrawn.
I've been stripped of more than my assets, boy.
I've paid the premiums, I am insured against that same old song.
You set my warning whistles wailing, sirens before the blaze.
Arsonist.
Romantic.
I know your wily, wafting ways, and I don't buy
sweet smelling come-ons,
not even on the budget plan.
I've held my feet to those flames before,
this time I'll stick to the frying pan.

Where I control the temperature,
no more broken heart attacks.
I don't want to burn the house down.

Still,
now and then,
I could use —
a wash and wax.

So, I'll bring along the prudence,
a bucket of icy water,
you grab your slippery, sweet-smellin' soap,
and we'll bubble up without the expectation,
the hand-holding, the soul searching,
the hope.
Two consenting adults,
hayrollers, in an oasis of cool design,
intimately not involved,
sharing a buff and shine.
That I can take — from time to time.

But don't be lighting any candles,
I won't open that valentine.
These days, I wear my running shoes to dance.
No more agonizing pain, no more sorrow, and
no combustible romance.
I'll take the lick without the promise.
Thank you.
You can keep the cheap cologne.
I want the house to still be standing
when I have to return to it
alone.

Eclipse

Advance notice
announced by someone,
sure, but not to me.
The eclipse broke the certain circle of the moon,
hanging back
behind the lake-heavy clouds,
shamefully, it seemed.
      Out of order.

Not seeking "new and different."
No telescope in my pocket.
No camera.
I was simply putting out the dog, following my feet
on their daily path. Routine. But I looked up, a glance.
The sighting, purely accidental.
Hardly enough to be sure.
      Might have pretended not to have seen it at all.

The next day news informs
that was the last lunar eclipse of the century.
And even though I ate raw vegetables today,
took my calcium, fresh water,
and one aspirin,
even though I walked, flossed
and wore my seatbelt, odds are best
      this century will see more of me than the next.

And if this was the last,
if this was the final of my century.
If this was the last time that life-worn pattern should be broken,
I almost wish I'd seen it on TV.
Or heard about it on the radio.
Or had someone send me a postcard, "Wish you were there,"
instead of bearing unsure witness.
   What earthly good?

I have no scrapbook of memories to recall,
no testimony to share.
Through this and into the next century,
I'll be sorting through this wondering of
if and what *was* that in the broken moonlight?
What. An eclipse?
Holding out on me like a longing love,
I felt — or maybe saw, but could not touch.
   Too hazy.
   So brief.

Again

Turned,
and once
you've seen it fleet away
and felt the rush of its escape.
Once you've purchased that
balloon and witnessed its deflate.
Once you've held by slender strings
the color burst of bliss,
experienced the loss,
cognizant of cost,
could you, by chance,
believe
a kiss
again?

Wedding Song

Well, look at both of you, all laced up and bow-tied.
Don't you look pretty. I mean it.
A picture of happiness in black and white.

I see you have quite a fire going here, mind if I warm my hands?
You kids headed downstream, are you?
Upstream?
Upstream?
Isn't that just like young folks. Upstream.
And you're taking all this stuff with you?
You sure got a lot of stuff.
Presents you say. Your inheritance.
Ain't it amazing what some folks'll dump on you, call it a gift.
I remember what I inherited from my folks.
An umbrella, my chin and a case of near terminal stubbornness.
The umbrella I lost right off.
The rest, I'm working on it.

I'd say you got some weighing out to do here.
Priorities.
What you going to take with you?
Helps to travel light, especially after all this
black and white turns to grey and grey.
What you going to take with you?
Just 'cause folks give you something, you know,
that doesn't mean you got to carry it the whole route.
You two get to decide, but, decide together.
That's the important part.
It's all these little decisions that
keep you going in the same direction.

I know, that seems to go without saying at this point
because it was your sameness, what you held in common,
that brought you together in the first place.
But what's going to keep you together
is how much gratitude you can find in your differences.

What you going to take with you?
Tell you one thing, you can't cut the mustard with a toaster.
As you're pondering and picking through this pile,
you remember:

Every luxury is a burden.
Every obligation you make separately, that's a chore.
Every plan you share, a pleasure.
Every gift of self, a joy.
Faith and trust will keep you afloat,
pride and bitterness can swamp you.
Resentments, those are the rocks to look out for.
And hang on, 'cause you're going to be
fighting the current the whole way.

Well, I better be going, leave the two of you alone.
Me and the rest of the folks here,
we'll be back in the morning.
We can't give you directions,
not one of us has been where you're going.
But just the same, we want to help you along,
just as far as we can.
So we'll be back.
Meantime, the two of you,
you mind the fire, you hear?
You mind the fire.

Written for the marriage of my daughter Kathleen Traynor,
November 1995

Truth be Known

Spring, we put the house on the market.
It was after that winter — we constructed a more tasteful kitchen?
Well, started the project and ran out of money, truth be known.
Had to keep the drapes drawn for four months.
We were certainly not very entertaining.
So no one really knew how torn up we were inside,
and I tell you this now in strictest confidence
only to underscore the fact that we were investing
all that we did not have in a major property value-added facelift,
taking utmost care that the seams would never show, very tasteful.
And in moves this new neighbor, a writer, we hear, two doors down.
In/out with that moving van
quicker than a seventeen-year-old in the back seat.

Next day I'm unloading tons of lite food from the station wagon
and along comes the new neighbor, walking his idiot brother.
Had the man by the hand, two grown men, can you imagine?
The idiot had on a magic marker red knit cap,
up one side, down the other on his too big head.
His inflated lips were fumbling soundlessly with the air
as he walked, draggin' one sidewise foot along,
like he just checked his shoes and was wiping the smell off.

That was the winter we all caught ringworm from the cat.
Imagine. No don't, you can catch it just thinking about it.
Doctor in another city, prescription in another county.
Covered the all-over red spots with turtlenecks,
catalog orders, to be sure, no dressing rooms, not in this town.
Little Natalie did develop one spot on her hand.
Had to have her whole arm mounted in a cast,
passed it off as a skiing accident, truth be known.

Truth be known, the winter wasn't all that bad compared to some
except for that new neighbor making me crazy with his idiot brother.
Everyday, fouling the atmosphere of our street.

Oh, don't tell me about what to call him that's politically correct.
The man's a blinking idiot. Clearly, this is what you would have
if Dickens had shopped for his characters at Kmart.
Wore his pants in four-inch cuffs rolled a good inch above his socks,
fat as a pregnant hippo, drooling and come to find out
when the weather began to warm? Big-eared and bald.
We maintain our own little ecosystem on this street,
a carefully balanced neighborhood
in a carefully balanced suburb and
we are all carefully balanced.
And then this new neighbor with his idiot brother,
who were all about upsetting things.

And I don't need to tell you how upset I was.
Why, that winter when our little Jimmy went into rehab we weren't
parading him up and down the sidewalks like some brassy band.
Or when Cynthia across the way ran off with the cableman,
her husband had a replacement unit snapped into the passenger side
of his Lexus quick and quiet as that little Japanese engine.
Why, even when Mr. Moore down the block
blew his brains out in February,
the ambulance came and went with no siren.
Which was why it frosted us all so much, that idiot and his brother,
everyday screaming their presence along our block.

But then came the final straw
and we put the house on the market next day.
We knew it was only a matter of time, truth be known.
Come to find out the new neighbor
wasn't any kind of legitimate writer at all.
He was a poet.

Free Lunch

Bent and staggered the man, like an onion,
could bring tears to the eyes,
shedding loose layers of gray stains,
trousers dragging a wake through the dust storm at his feet,
his eyes fixed on another place.
Indigenous to this landscape,
pungent, swaying in the morning stillness.
"He can't help it, he's homeless."
Child to adult, native to foreigner,
she explains to me, the day traveler.
I've been schooled to take the long view past his kind.
Only eight years old, she takes the short view.
She knows I am out of place, that I am in need of educating.
What kind of place I come from, she does not know,
She sees me exiting my car everyday and
assumes my place is different. She is right.

She is overflowing with last night's bedtime story.
How some guy tried to break in, how her dad stuck a shotgun
through the screen door, knocked out the bad guy's teeth.
Later, six eight-year-olds hold a cabinet meeting
to decide if dad should have blown the guy's head off,
would the blast have raised him off his feet,
how far the pieces would have scattered.

Thinking of my night, last night, there were clearly stars,
unencumbered, just a hang nail of a moon,
sounds of leaves mixing it up overhead.
I walked the dog.

Kids in my place,
during storms, they count the seconds between
the lightning and the thunder to help keep the scared away.
Here, kids count the hours between the gun shots and the sirens
and the storm and the scared never goes.
In my place, bathtubs are where you go to get clean.
Here, clean is what you want in a mom
and bathtubs are a place to get out of the crossfire.

She stamps my passport with a smile
and helps me with my bag.
Together, we climb into the trash can, metal rattlings
all around, foot-jammed full of yesterday's promises,
wrapped up in the same old news,
a gathering place for roaches and rats,
battleworn, sagging and bruised.
For lack of another term, we call it school.
And funnier still, sometimes they call me teacher.

Kids in my neighborhood come to school
with their backpacks stuffed with lunches and supplies.
Here, the kids arrive empty-handed,
heavily laden with knowing —
knowing how to conjugate cockroach.
Knowing how to calculate time served.
Knowing just about everything there is to know about
how folks multiply and divide.
All of these tomorrows being fed nothing but leftovers.
Kids in this place will tell you straight out.
There ain't no such thing as a free lunch.
I stand at the classroom window
and see the man still stationed at the corner.
Today's lesson.
He can't help it, you know. He's homeless.

Do You Care to Comment?

How'd you like to bear a child,
soon's you lay that sweet dew drop down' the crib,
the roaches be skittering in to nibble his soul?
You try and shew 'em off but you can't.
You can't.
And you can't go back to Kentucky 'cause that road lead but one way,
and you got no place to go. You got no work place.
No going out place. You got but this place,
where you can't even shut your eyes for the skittering.
Till one day you look and all the meat's all gone,
there ain't nothing left but some rancid gravy running out the slats.
You try and catch that with your fingers, but it run on through
till you got nothing left you but a spot on the ground.

My boy jumped off the roof of the Towers.
He found out he got AIDS and the TV news people, they's everywhere.
Skittering. So dyin' big news. Today.
Weren't no big news when my boy outta school
runnin' with them hoods.
That suicide without the ledge.
Where the news when he took his first needle?
That suicide, not about to see that at no six o'clock.
No pretty hairdo straddling the needle scars spiderwebbin' they way
up his arm like she done the scar he made out the parking lot.
Where the news then?

Do I care to comment?
News media, y'all flock around here like birds discussing travel plans.
You don't know news.

Do I care to comment?
'Bout what? Ain't nothin' new here.
Here's what they call, "lake effect," where the breeze off the lake
smell like exhaust, air's moving, just churning up ol' dirt.

Do I care to comment?
You try and raise kids right 'round here.
Can't even let them out to play for the crossfire.
Why, the whores be doing their dirt in the hall outside our door.
Our home.
No use calling the police, time they gets there, if they gets there,
it's over and me left answerin' questions
no chil' ought have words for.
You want to explain a open-mouth whore facing an open fly
to an open-eyed chil' not tall enough to reach a swing yet?
Where the news then? Let me ask you.
Do you care to comment?

And don't you call me welfare mother, neither,
'cause it ain't my mothering needs subsidy, it's this place here.
I surely wants more for my chil' than I got for myself;
that is the mother instinct, and I got news for y'all,
mother instinct, it don't cost nothin'.
Rich or poor, you's either born with it or you ain't.

So, you stop your skittering, y'hear?
The meat's all gone, done run through my fingers long time ago.
Ain't nothin' new here.
Over yonder, there's your story.
Ain't nobody interested in my comment or my boy killin' hisself.
All's they's interested in's his blood spot.
You go'n get it now.
There
is your big news.

The Gardener

I work the city garden plot as best I can.
I got to be feedin' it, feedin' it all the time.
The soil's just starved.

Soil filled with wild grasses,
greens and wild flowers, milkweed,
it never gets wore out.
Year after year, busts out in every direction,
alive, roots all intertwined,
protecting the soil.
Each generation giving life to the next.

Man comes along, he separates nature into rows.
Corn here, wheat there, tobacco, beans,
and he plots the soil's demise.
Does his best to kill off the natural
mingling of growth that keeps the soil rich.
Man does.

Some will tell you it works out,
since we all wind up in the same ground eventually,
death being democratic like it is.
Man, plant and beast, side by side.
'Course, even then we put ourselves in boxes.
Man does.

Little Sister

My mama, she told me, "Be careful."
The boy, he told me he loved me.

The teacher said, "Don't be a fool. You stay in school."
The boy, he told me he loved me.

The TV said, "Practice safe sex."
The boy, he told me he loved me.

My daddy said, "You get pregnant, I'm gonna kick you out."
The boy, he told me he loved me.

Stepping Out

The world made room for you, babies,
your toothless grins and charms,
clapped when you took first steps
and held you in privileged arms.

Such a magical reception!
Trees turned into cribs and diapers and announcements.
"Voila!" exclaimed the world.
"These babies will need bibs,
and vitamins and formula,
and pint-sized tube socks for their toes.
These babies will need central heat.
These babies, it said,
"Not those."

Presto! Pigs turned into hot dogs.
Cows into burgers and sneaker leather.
Geese and sheep gave up their coats
to protect you from Cleveland weather.
Water turned into colas.
Potatoes into chips.
Rocks turned into fuel
to propel you on your trips
to malls and work and school.

Then, the world taxed all your neighbors
so you could learn, but second hand,
all about starvation,
about deprivation,
about dictators and war.
The goblins of the world, viewed through
a media peephole in a sturdy suburban door.

We know.
No one asked you if this was fair,
to be raised on top-shelf milk.
The world will ask you for answers,
but the question is not guilt.

It's privilege.
Is it just a blessing?
A responsibility?
A maze of social traps?
An isolationist position?
Or is it just, perhaps,
a gilded invitation to help
construct a place
where less is more,
where more costs less
and where more babies can be safe.

The world made room for you,
when it was crowded and hungry and tired,
hoping, one day, that comfort
would grow uncomfortable.
That one day you'd grow
inspired to find solutions.
The world gave you the strength
to seek that *something else,*
and to stand up to
the nonchalance of privilege
as now, you step out
to make room for yourself.

*Written for my daughter Kelly Traynor Weist and
the graduates of Bay High School Class of 1993.*

Which Road?

Good Lord.
Praise be.
Thank God.
You're not like other men.
I know this, Love, you told me, and I can't be fooled again.

You travel about my cheek with fingertips too soft for other men.
You're caring and a listener.
Your wife is still your friend.
You have drive, but you're not driven.
Competition's not your game.
It's just great that I'm successful, no need for playoffs,
why, we're practically the same.
Both wear deodorant for sensitive skin.
Both of us can cry. Of course, you've never strayed before.
Why would either of us lie?

You breathe your kiss into my lips with tenderness,
you're not like all the rest.
You hate hockey, football, blond jokes.
You love intelligence, small breasts.
You despise those other men who live to hunt and belch and spit.
You crave cuddling, cozy fires, shooting stars, and candles,
both ends lit.
You want a woman whose eyes crinkle with experience,
who knows not to call the house.
You make a sincere attempt at eye contact
with every button on my blouse
explaining you love poetry, ballet, your heart and soul are giving.
You don't like those younger women, who want babies
and can't even make a living on their own.

What fun is that?
You're never free at home and they're never free to travel.
You warn them to watch their hearts, but then they snap
and just unravel when you leave and don't return.
Oh, yes.
I know them.
I know how they cry and ache and yearn.
I know how many of those other men they'll have to know
before they learn.

Not like you, oh, you'd never break my heart.
Never leave me low or reeling, unanswered, disappointed
beard-burned, bruised, diseased, or peeling.
Oh, no.
I'm tough and wise and wonderful. You told me so, I'm different, too.
Not at all like her, a mouth so full of bitters she can't give good
understanding like I do.

My Love, you're not like other men, and I can't be fooled again.
So who cares if you put out the trash.
What we have is more real than that.
It could never get tied down by debt
before you grab your jeans and baseball hat.
And though I may have cats and lacy curtains,
I can tell you this with just a sigh,
no need to bash or hiss and yell.
You're right.
I'm not like other women, Love.
I am a poet.
I kiss and tell.

And that has made all the difference.

Parlor Games

Lock that door,
squeaks the recluse pushing her heels into the floor,
her straight back matching the chair — rock for rock.
Grounded again, held inside by her stern stare,
I turn on the radio so I can't hear her sucking the bones.
That's enough, she screams. *No more.*
There will be no more jazz.
I nod like the clown in the back window of a car
driven by someone else. I click the radio off.
You should have known better.
I know. I know.
You should have known.
I know.
I told you so.
Yes ma'm.
I'll agree to anything to stop that predictable squeak.
I'll button my collar to the neck.
I'll make prayer hands in my lap.
I'll rock in perfect imitation, waiting.
Yes, I know and she's right. Of course she's right. I know.
I know she'll fall off. Satisfaction will make her tired.
I hum softly to myself and watch for her chest to fold in,
her head to drop. I watch for the heavy eyes.
As soon as her tight jaw begins to slack, I will make my move.
I'll sneak like a dream to tie the laces together on her sensible shoes,
crawl under the table and unlock the door.
No more jazz.
I know. I know.
I don't want to tell you again.
I know.
Stop that humming.
Yes ma'm.

Keep or Toss

It's a sleep-late Sunday — afternoon,
and almost time for dinner.
With no pressing debts and two hours free to spend,
I sit here figuring. What to do?

Could translate Beowulf from Old English.
Could swim to Canada.
Could clean out my garage.
Tasks equally formidable.
I fumble around in options while playing keep or toss
with a catch-all basket on my desk.
Overflowing.

In the basket, a couple bills — keep.
Advertisements — toss.
A lipstick, pens, a comb.
A sharp jab, I quick suck a dab of blood from the assaulted finger,
poised then, chin to thumb for remembering.
Other needles hugged by former fingers,
small and fumbly, thimble always protecting the wrong tip.

It was my Granny who taught me to sew,
to visualize the possibilities of gingham and corduroy,
so much cheaper than wool.
My first lesson in economics.
To measure twice and cut once.
And since the future is certain to arrive undressed,
to save all your scraps, for lining pockets, patching knees
and for quilting.

Granny, who never sat at Sunday dinner,
too busy serving us, who never sat in the living room
where the men discussed politics,
who never earned a wage for all her work at home,
for friends, family or the First Methodist Church,
the fixed fencing that encircled her days.
She took life like dictation and hummed while she worked.

Granny always knew what to do with a Sunday.
Fry it up early, drain off the fat for later pans,
serve it, wash it, dress it up in clothes stirred and pressed
into starched attention that past Tuesday.
Worship it, cook and serve it up big again at noon
on china prized for its age.
Maybe join it for a nap, a supper, a walk and bed it down by 8:30.

This afternoon my daughter sits, one of Granny's quilts
wrapped about her knees, flipping through catalogs for
tomorrow's laundry, sneakers propped on an antique tool chest,
empty now, channel selector in hand.
              Click — a movie.
              Click — a game.
              Click — Click.
Her first response to boredom.
              Click — Click.
And the infinite choices of a life
              Click —
without
              Click
preconstructed definitions.
Eating off a paper napkin, drinking pop from disposable bottles.
Depositing today's scraps into the trash,
which I will later separate for recycling.
Playing keep — or toss.

Common Ground

"Hey, what is it with white folks and tattoos?"
She began, spreading her napkin on her lap
under a warm grin, nodding pointedly at a passing arm
drawn about the biceps with lacy blue vines.
She took up the stemmed water glass, her eyes lit with laughter,
a clatter of ice against the glass as she took a sip.
It was one of those lunches,
scheduled not sometime, but now.

"I don't know," I answered,
opening a menu, skimming the options.
"What is it with black folks and gold jewelry?"
I tipped my head to the side,
a shining example ear-looped and dangling at the next table.
It was a let's get to know one another,
I like your humor and intellect,
can we find a place outside of the office,
a place, a little too formal,
to be our best selves, see if we can find friendship.
It was that kind of lunch.

Orders made, iced tea served,
lemon slices tipped at a jaunty angle.
Talk of schools, siblings, all the wherefroms.
The entrees circled and landed.
Would there be anything else?
No we'd be fine. Two women,
both accustomed to management,
no problem speaking our minds.

"So, what is it with white folks and their therapists?"
A question. I paused, fork on the way up,
then took in the bite and chewed in silence.
A questioning response.
She replied, "Little girl in my department,
her daddy died and her husband run off.
Now she's taking sick time,
dragging her whiny self off to some shrink for depression.
My mama worked cleaning white folks houses
five bucks a day everyday of her life,
me watching the other four kids.
Everyday, the five bucks went for clothes,
food, and a little bit in the rent envelope.
No time for vacation, no school program.
No work, no five bucks.
Depression."
She vigorously speared an innocent lettuce leaf.
"What the shit is that."

Smoothing the tablecloth
in front of my plate as if it were wrinkled,
I picked up my knife and moving with even precision,
sawed into the meat.
"What is it with black women together?"
She hesitated and lowered her eyebrows.
"I have been working six months in the same office
with you and your friends,
not once has anyone asked me to lunch."
She stared and chewed twice, still holding her fork mid-air,

"Well, my hand's on this damned fork
and my butt's in this chair,"
she pointed from here to there,
"I guess you could say this is lunch."
Her neck followed her head side to side
as she lay her words on the table one at a time.
"Yeah, but I asked you
and you snuck that butt out the back door to meet me outside."
I wiped my mouth. "I was born late but not stupid, you know."

"And white folks don't stick together, I suppose."
Our accusations met head on.
"I got plenty to take care of in that office,"
she leaned confidentially into her comments,
"I don't need to be tending after your sensitivities."
"Nobody needs to tend after me," I answered,
"I am not some Scarlett O'Hara,"
and I inflamed with just that color.
"Yeah, and I'm not your Aunt Jemima."
She sat back and folded her arms.

Paying our separate checks, we prepared to walk back to the office,
each holding up our end of the silence.
Waiting for a too long traffic light,
a Camaro roared past, leaving wide, dual wakes of dust and exhaust.
We brushed the loose dirt from our skirts.

"Hey," she said breaking the roaring silence,
"What is it with men and those cars?"
"You know why they need all that muscle under the hood?"
I tipped her elbow with mine, nodding at the changing light.
"Not enough muscle under the belt,"
she replied and stepped into the crosswalk.
We laughed our way back to the office,
stretching our legs across common ground.

Playing in Traffic

A city
in traffic,
a panic
of isolate screams,
captured inside
exhaust machines,
on lanes that like tracks
hold cars to their courses
to offices, shops
reunions, divorces.
HORNS
speaking their minds.
Emotions at large,
stampeding to
radios
tuned to the charge.

Last Spring

If it were last spring,
you and I would walk
that path again
beside the rushing water,
trading stories,
risking the slipperiness of mud,
offering each other a hand
instead of warnings,
wistful fingers
touching tip to root,
turning palm to sun
in rapt absorption,
long days coming,
promising their berries
fair payment for time served.

Last spring,
the ground stripped free
of all this knowing,
the summer's bountiful harvest
of fact.

I wish we could go back.

What a Picture!

Here stands the bridal party
on the manmade steps of this stone church,
at the entrance to the sanctity of marriage.
The groom, straight and swift as a javelin.
The bride, a chiffon blossom with a bouquet at her center.
The entire picture framed by fresh flowers, natural fragrances,
for nothing is simply manmade.
Nature will always find its way.

The rest of us gaze on the picture and exclaim:
How beautiful! What promise!
This must have cost a fortune!
And don't we know it did,
in amounts for which there is no currency exchange.
Today we pause and add up these rememberings,
how both of you were born,
standouts, little dandelions, growing freely, spindly,
bright as sunshine, and both a wee bit stubborn.
Oh, we remember, determined to go your own way.
Two distinct individuals,
fed by your families, not on or by demand,
with love.
Freely.

It is the manmade world that stipulates, designates,
with deadlines, long lines, lines drawn in the sand.
Its driving, Dervish, dancing beat demands.
Demands.
While love, love is a lilting bird song,
a gentle beckoning so sweet, never a demand note.

It draws us to its heart as it has drawn the two of you
to the manmade steps of this stone church,
no longer two apart, but two like so many others.
Coupling. But what cost this fusion?
Are you to be forever trapped by these stone walls?
Will you be robbed of the distinction that is your birthright?
Does marriage mute the carefully nurtured individual voice?

All the trappings in the world cannot set you apart from nature
unless you've lost your way. So, look to the river.
Is it merely confined by its banks,
or do those banks help speed it toward the sea?
Like the river, you will always know inner freedom
if you know which way you're headed.
If together you can say no to the demands of the world
in favor of your common destination, moving forward,
knowing that to hurt the other is to hurt your progress and yourself.
That harmony takes two voices.
That love is the ultimate joy, a destination no one can find alone.

The rest of us rememberers, we are here by invitation,
you two are here by choice. And from this day on, your freedom
will be expressed by your choosing to move forward together —
Today, tomorrow — toward that common joy.
Know that every blossom, in nature, has a purpose.
And listen, listen for the birdsong:

> From love are born all creatures, by love they are sustained,
> towards love they progress, and into love they enter.

As naturally as water,
love will always find its way.

Written for the wedding of my daughter Kelly Traynor and Brian Weist.
August 9, 1997. Quote from Rabindranath Tagore, Sadhana, The
Realisation of Life *(1914).*

Undated

A sweet topping
to the conversation,
my touch against your brow
to smooth a crevice that
some care had trailed
across your forehead.
Just a touch
without intentions,
as I would dust
a hair
from my own eye.

Your hand upon my hip,
was it then?
Or was it later?
Later still,
I can't recall.

Intimacy brushes,
brief happens and forgottens.
Undated —
just a memory
of the quick twist,
your cheek then chin
as you so slightly closed your eyes
and leaned into my palm
for that one touch.

Still Looking

I am looking
for that place
beyond resign
and cope,
where promise can ignite
and wishing can
find hope.
Where the downside
knows its place,
desires don't
do without,
and happiness can't hear
the whimpering
of doubt.

Learning Center
Twin Groves Junior High School
2600 Buffalo Grove Rd.
Buffalo Grove, IL. 60089

DISCARD